WESTERN IMPRESSIONS

Photo by Mira Atkeson

DEDICATION

To my wife Mira, who was my inspiration, helpmate, expert evaluator, and more than any man could hope for in many other ways during our 45 years of married life.

Together we enjoyed our travels throughout the West exploring the beauty along highways, byways, wilderness trails, scrambling through miles of pathless forests. We thrilled to exciting sights and experiences during trips abroad, and endured the hardships and frustrations that are part of a serious pictorial photographer's life, just as our two spirits responded with delight when conditions were most favorable for capturing on film the beauty and majesty of the great outdoors.

Mira was a talented and creative photographer in her own right. Outstanding volumes of her pictorial nature photography could be published, but her activities in this mutually shared field of endeavor were directed toward organizational and service work, in addition to competition in camera clubs.

As a competitor, Mira won many local and international honors, medals, and trophies, the most recent being the coveted A.P.S.A. honor given her by the Photographic Society of America.

Without Mira's companionship and encouragement during the years when the going was rough, it is unlikely that this or any of the other published books of my work would have seen the light of day. My greatest pleasure and good fortune has been the experience of our life together.

Her presence will be sorely missed not only by me but by countless other people who knew her. She contributed more than her share toward making the world a better place for the rest of us to live in.

WESTERN IMPRESSIONS

Photographed by

RAY ATKESON

WESTERN IMPRESSIONS

Contents

Second Printing, June 1977

Published by Beautiful West Publishing Company
202 N.W. 21st Avenue
Portland, Oregon 97209

Publisher, Robert D. Shangle

Printed in the United States of America

Lithography by Fremont Litho Inc., Fremont, California

SBN 0-915796-11-2

Preface

My love affair with the West and the great outdoors is probably hereditary. My father had an uncontrollable wanderlust that lured him on prospecting trips through Arizona and other western states when the West was really the "Wild West" of historical fact and fiction. After he married my mother, he built his house atop a prominent viewpoint on his 320-acre farm overlooking wooded canyons that reached down to the Illinois River near its confluence with the Mississippi. The grand panorama we had across the Illinois, Mississippi, and the distant Missouri is still vivid in my memory, as is the roar of storms sweeping up across the oak forests, the rain and hail audible on dry foliage long before it reached us. I remember lonely but exciting explorations in snake-infested canyons searching for Indian artifacts and fool's gold that protruded from slate cliffs or had been loosened and washed down into creek beds. That farm is now included in an Illinois State Park.

My western experience didn't begin until after high school graduation in 1924 when newspaper headlines called for 24,000 workers to harvest a bumper wheat crop in Kansas. My mother operated a dry-goods store in Kansas City at that time, and, not really meaning it, I told her I wished I could go to the harvest fields. I was completely flabbergasted and a bit alarmed when she answered: "Well, why don't you go?"

A week later my closest friend and I were riding the top of a freight train with hundreds of burly harvest hands and bums heading for western Kansas. Every freight west out of Kansas City was similarly adorned. We two 135-pound tenderfoot kids found ourselves among thousands of rugged veterans in Hutchinson, Kansas, only to learn that harvest was still a week or more away.

We heard a rumor that harvest was ready to begin a hundred miles to the west, so we spent the rest of our meager cash for passenger train tickets to Ness City. We were among a hundred or more first on the scene, and to our amazement one of the farmers asked us if we wanted a job. He had a family of young children and apparently decided to take a chance on us rather than the tougher, experienced hands. I will always remember the first week of 10-hour days in the field. We didn't earn our salt, but the family and food were great, and when the crop was harvested we headed on west with more confidence and fewer blisters. We finally returned home through Nebraska with fifteen more pounds — all muscle — on our frames and a lot of cash.

That and two more summers in the harvest fields of Kansas, Colorado, Nebraska, and South Dakota were filled with experiences that might make interesting reading, but it was my first view of the Front Range of the Rockies, far to the west, that remains most vivid in my memory. One summer we took time to explore some of that Front Range before continuing our work as migrants on ranches and wheat farms.

The third summer's harvest was only a means of getting farther west, into and through the Rockies. Across the desert between Colorado and Green River, Utah — only a couple hours' drive now — was for us a day of twelve flat tires that had to be repatched and

repumped in 120-degree temperatures. In Green River, Utah, we bought a "five-minute" heat vulcanizer with which we replaced the cold patches and solved that particular problem.

To the west we traversed some rugged canyons and redrock country I've never located again during my many trips through the area. But since there is plenty of such terrain all over southern Utah and Arizona, I've never really searched very hard for that old route we crossed.

Bryce Canyon, Zion National Park, and Cedar Breaks were even more beautiful than we could have imagined. With some concern we headed for the coast through Las Vegas and across the Mojave Desert, traveling only at night as other travelers advised us, to escape the furnace-like, daytime heat. Our only problem was occasionally losing the road while crossing sand drifts that covered the highway in places. Paved roads and gas stations were scarce in the 1920s.

It was a thrill for us just to be in California after having heard so much about its countless wonders. However, we still hadn't reached our goal of Portland, Oregon, and weren't quite sure we ever wanted to come to the end of our nomadic life. Mt. Shasta changed all that — at least temporarily. When we got to its base, we thought, "This is the place." We decided to tarry and fortunately landed a job in a box factory right at the foot of the massive 14,000-foot volcanic peak. We spent our spare time exploring the surrounding area, and on Labor Day weekend we even trudged up to Shasta's summit. It was a long grind to timberline at 8,000 feet and the mountain above was difficult so late in the year because we were climbing over boulders and loose rock instead of the snowfields of early summer. But we were young and in good physical condition and knew nothing about mountain climbing. It was a grand experience.

A few days later the box factory burned to the ground, leaving us jobless. With a new friend I again headed north. After some short prune-harvesting jobs, we worked in a logging camp near Ryderwood, Washington, but that was a short job, too. Then we decided to try apple-picking in Hood River Valley, Oregon. The crop was good that year and we did well.

One morning, after a night of heavy rain, we looked out of our hillside cabin and saw Mt. Adams in Washington all decked out in a new robe of snow. The orchard was too drenched for apple picking so we set out in the old Ford to explore. That day's wandering took us up a narrow, slick, forest-bound road toward Lost Lake. After a lot of sliding, slithering, and pushing we reached the lake.

I was hooked for life. The Northwest, I decided, was the end of the trail for me. Mt. Hood and Lost Lake have never seemed more beautiful to me than that first sight of them, and I've been there countless times since. The peak was gleaming white with new snow, its image reflected by the mirror surface of the lake. And we had it all to ourselves.

After the apple crop was harvested, my friend went home to Long Beach, California, and I stayed in Portland. Jobs were practically non-existent and the only work I could find was as a door-to-door magazine salesman. It was work I detested and my sales reflected my lack of enthusiasm. A member of the magazine crew took me home to dinner one night where I met his mother and his sister, Mira, who later became Mira Atkeson. I finished that rainy winter making a living and no more, and had to sell my car. After this I decided to look for work in California. A new friend and I bought another old car and we hit the road; no time schedule and no money, only credentials from a publishing company and a desire to see more of the West.

Our car, credentials, stock of magazines, and clothing were stolen at Phoenix, so we just struck out eastward, traveling mostly by ore trains from the mining country, and hitch-hiking. The West didn't seem so glamorous after three consecutive foodless days and sleep-less nights on the way home to Kansas City, where I visited for a few days.

Mira and the West proved too much of a lure, and with $11 in my pocket I once more headed west, hitch-hiking again. Portland was a welcome sight for many reasons. Mira and I discovered mutual interests, and we especially enjoyed the great outdoors of Oregon and Washington. However, it was a long time before our jobs per-mitted extensive exploratory trips. This was 1928-1929. Depression time. The work week for the fortunate job-holders was six full days, usually from 8 a.m. to 6 p.m., and sometimes longer. That left only one day for rest and recreation, in our case trail hiking and mountain climbing. We did manage to spend a week on a trip to the coast in the old second-hand car I owned then. Mira, her mother, a cousin, and I shared the adventures and pleasures of the trip. In that era the coast road was dirt interrupted by long, narrow stretches of corduroy (planks and logs) laid across extra boggy areas. The road took long detours around bays and stream outlets.

It wasn't long before we were married. We continued to enjoy our hikes and climbs with friends who had the same calling. A group of five of us were on a winter sunrise hike from Multnomah Falls to the rocky summit of Larch Mountain when we decided to organize. At first we called ourselves the Columbian Hikers, but later changed the name to Wy'east Climbers (Wy'east is Mt. Hood's Indian name). A few ambitious members were added and our adventures expanded. Glacier exploration became our favorite activity.

I had a new job with a small commercial photo studio, and a camera became an integral part of my equipment on all our trips. Saturday nights were spent traveling and hiking or climbing to our destination. Sundays were days of exploration and, for me, photog-raphy was now a major interest.

Climbs of major peaks in those days took a bit longer than they do now. For instance, we had to hike from Government Camp to Mt. Hood's summit, and once when our car broke down, we hiked seven or eight miles to Timberline to start the climb. Another time, two companions and I reached the summit from Government Camp in five hours. But that wasn't my idea of climbing. I preferred a more leisurely style, for exploration and enjoyment.

Skiing, if it can be called that, was another activity for our group long before it became so popular. Usually we skied up to Timberline by wrapping clothes-line rope around the skis for traction. Then, after some frolicking on the open snowfields, we would make our unskilled descent as best we could.

One January in the early 1930s Mira and I and two friends, Ralph Calkens and Ole Lein, spent a week holed up in the decrepit old Camp Blossom cabin at Timberline while blizzards blew outside. It was short on comfort, but it was at least a shelter. Finally the long siege broke and we set out before dawn in clear, cold weather for a climb to the summit. Deep new snow made it rugged going but we reached the top. The summit cliffs and ridge were a fantastic spectacle and my camera captured some striking photos. I believe Mira was one of the first women to climb the mountain in winter. I made other winter climbs of the peak in ensuing years.

I found an enthusiastic market for my photos from our explora-tions and adventures. Newspaper rotogravure sections and magazines all over the nation published full-page and double-page spreads of my work. It was inspiration and a great help in providing much needed funds in those trying times so that we could continue our trips.

Mira took time out to add to the family, our daughter Eleanor, and it wasn't long before she was accompanying us. Sometimes I wonder if we were very considerate of her wishes, but she never complained. She added a new dimension to our vacations, frequently modeling in my scenic pictures and enjoying the beauty of nature as it was revealed to her.

In 1946 free-lance outdoor photography became a full-time profession for me. Assignments from many national magazines and advertising agencies took me to far-away and out-of-the-way places and resulted in a greatly expanded library of photos.

This book is not intended as a geographical coverage of the West. For various reasons some outstanding spectacles of the West are not included in this collection. Others may be represented more than once. One volume can only include a small fraction of my more vivid impressions. The West is vast and varied. The majesty of mighty mountains and the rugged coastlines are only a part of the settings that dominate with their beauty; but they are no more beautiful and impressive than the more intimate life on the forest floor or in the desert sands.

The West, along with the rest of the world, is constantly changing. Many of those changes by man have destroyed beauty and harmony. But some may be an improvement on the original natural environ-ment. Without roads some of nature's beauty would be totally inaccessible for millions of aged and handicapped people. Without power, life itself would be less pleasant for most of us. Without timber harvest, how would we all be sheltered? But a great deal more consideration of the potential effect on environment should be a part of all plans for change.

In very recent years, many politicians and industrialists have become more conscious of their obligation to the future. Whether this awareness has been voluntarily incorporated into their activities or forced on them by the ever-increasing pressure of conservation-oriented individuals and organizations, I believe the thoughtless desecration of our natural environment will continue to decrease and that our West and other beautiful areas of the world will continue to be good places to live.

A Navajo Indian whose ancestors were among the first human inhabitants of the West.

(Overleaf) In the beginning almost constant volcanic activity created vast lava flows and mountain peaks. Some are small like this one photographed on the youthful Island of Hawaii. Others are tremendous in height and size.

As time passed volcanoes on the mainland ceased their activity. Other changes took place. Some of the land lay beneath the sea. As the land rose again and the water receded, in places like Monument Valley the most durable stone remained towering above surrounding desert valleys.

The sea relentlessly continues to attack and erode the land. This dramatic surf action was photographed at the foot of the Na Pali Cliffs of Kauai Island, Hawaii.

Eventually life came to the West. Plants like this columbine took root in the soil, multiplied in number and variety, and burst into bloom.

Giant trees grew and forests spread over some of the land where abundant moisture nourished them.

The forests reach from seashore, valleys, and mountain ranges to high elevations where climatic conditions are severe. The growth reluctantly comes to a gradual halt, leaving only the most hardy trees to band together in tight clusters for survival at timberline.

With plant life, other life came to the West. Birds and animals of many kinds in countless numbers roam forests and desert land. Here waterfowl fill the sky at Tule Lake National Wildlife Refuge in northern California.

Then came man. Here a catamaran drops anchor on a Hawaiian shoreline, a scene reminiscent of the landing of the first Hawaiians after their voyage across the South Pacific.

The West is varied in character, as varied as its geology and climatic conditions. Here in semi-arid southern Utah the Escalante River water and sand reflect the glow of sunset still illuminating canyon walls.

A band of sheep rest contentedly in a setting of golden autumn beauty in Pleasant Valley, southwestern Colorado.

Hidden Lake nestles in a pocket at the foot of rugged mountains scoured by glaciers of the Ice Age in Glacier National Park, Montana.

A fresh blanket of snow in early autumn covers the 12,326 foot volcanic cone of Mt. Adams in the Cascade Range in southern Washington.

Lower Proxy Falls pours a veil of water over a high cliff in the Three Sisters Wilderness in the Central Cascade Range of Oregon. Spray from the falls nourishes green moss on boulders and logs at its base.

The Three Sisters Wilderness in the central Cascade Range of Oregon lies dormant beneath deep snow that blankets the high volcanic peaks and glaciers in winter.

California poppies bloom in a green field at the base of a wind-sculptured oak tree in the Santa Ynez Valley.

(Overleaf) Colorful sandstone cliffs of Cape Kiwanda in Oregon contrast dramatically with relentless storm clouds and dark Pacific surf.

Early morning sunlight sparkles from frost-fringed vegetation at the edge of an aspen grove in Sun Valley, Idaho.

Palm trees at Waikiki sway in the evening breeze as sunset glow spreads across the Hawaiian sky.

Vine maple foliage stages perhaps the most colorful display of all Northwestern native plants during the autumn season. Vine maple grows most prolifically in forest regions of western Oregon and Washington.

One of the highest and most spectacular of all the volcanic mountains in the Cascade Range is Glacier Peak in the heart of the Glacier Peak Wilderness in northwestern Washington, penetrated only by trail.

Lehman Caves National Monument at the base of Wheeler Peak in east central Nevada is one of the most colorful and interesting caverns in America.

Golden, autumn-tinted aspen foliage is photographed against a Wyoming sagebrush-covered hillside shrouded in late afternoon shadows.

New autumn snow at timberline gives warning that this spike buck should consider retreating to the protection of forests at lower elevations.

The Southwest

Long before my travels took me westward, I was more familiar with the Southwest region than might have been expected. I had moved to Kansas City, Missouri, and the beginning of my sophomore year was "get acquainted day" in my new English class. I was a bit too naive, honest, or ignorant in answering the Number One question put to us by the teacher: "Who is your favorite author?" My reply was Zane Grey; other pupils mentioned Shakespeare, etc. Well, I really got a reaming out, and I was never permitted to forget that honest answer all during that class year.

Whatever my favorite author's qualifications may or may not have been, he wasn't at the top of Miss Begbie's list of writers. Even so, the dean of all Western fiction writers had a way with words. His knowledge of his subject could not be questioned, and his description of the land and people about which he wrote was so vivid that the reader was seemingly transported into the story so effectively that the scent of pine forests, terrifying electrical storms reverberating in the canyons, the heat of desert wastes, beauty of the redrock country, every canyon, stream, trail, and countless details, as well as the overall grandeur were indelibly impressed in the mind of the reader. So it was with me.

The Tonto Rim, Rainbow Trail, outlaw hideouts, real or fancied, were as familiar to me as if I had already been there, long before I finally had the opportunity to actually see and travel through that fantastic region.

By that time many changes had taken place, but my impressions gained from my avid reading of Zane Grey's novels proved to be amazingly close to what I expected. I found myself visualizing the characters of his books pursuing their activities, living the rugged ranch life, riding the trails and open spaces, even trying to avoid the treacherous needles of cactus plants. I imagined the possibilities for hideaways in the deep remote areas of the redrock country where countless caves, weathered in sandstone cliffs, provided shelter for their headquarters.

Few places in the world project the vastness that is so impressive in the redrock country of Utah and Arizona, even in this modern age. Highways have, of course, woven a limited network across the region. Off-road vehicles roar through wild areas formerly traversed only on foot or horseback. In the wilds of New Mexico, Utah, Colorado, and Arizona rivers have been tamed by dams, settlements have grown, and even the famed azure-blue sky is smudged by the smoke of industry, especially the smoke of mammoth coal-burning power plants.

Fortunately, a high percentage of this vast Southwest wonderland has been preserved by establishment of numerous national parks and national monuments, which should result in protection that will assure minimum unwise development and discourage vandalism, intentional or otherwise. Some former national monuments have in the mid 70s been changed to national park status. Controls have been established in popular but fragile areas so as to prevent erosion triggered by off-road vehicle traffic.

We can only visualize in our minds the former natural beauty of green vegetation, of eroded rocks polished by flood waters and lying on the dark floors of the Colorado River Canyon and its tributary canyons, all now lying buried beneath the deep, calm water of Lake Powell, created by Glen Canyon Dam. Our conception of what once existed can be sharpened if we study the magnificent photos of Eliot Porter published in the Sierra Club book, **Glen Canyon, The Place No One Knew**.

Here along the Colorado River has been wrought perhaps the greatest man-made change in the vast Southwest region in recent history. It surely is the most controversial. Now we have a mammoth lake with an 1,800-mile shoreline reaching far back into deep tributary canyons and desert valleys. A lake that is beautiful with its vivid blue waters, surrounded by colorful redrock towers, walls, and mesas. It's true that thousands of people can now enjoy the beauty of the lake and region by boat or from the air, whereas not many years ago only a few hardy individuals or groups had the privilege of hiking and camping among the trees and shrubs on the floor of the canyon.

Promises of politicians and engineers, like Indian treaties, seem to be made only to be broken. During the Glen Canyon controversy, fabulous Rainbow Bridge, one of the natural wonders of the world, located in a tributary canyon about five miles from the Colorado, was to be forever protected from erosion of the lake water. One excuse after another has resulted in no real assurance that Rainbow Bridge will not be destroyed by undermining action of the water which has reached the base of the bridge. Already a desperate situation exists.

It had long been my desire to see Rainbow Bridge and the Rainbow Trail. I finally made that dream become a reality long before Glen Canyon Dam and Lake Powell existed.

My impressions on that long trail trip which started at Rainbow Lodge, Arizona, on the south shoulder of Navajo Mountain are impossible to convey by word or pictures. Navajo Mountain itself dominates the horizon of the Southwest region for perhaps a hundred miles. It loses none of its interest with familiarity.

The trail traverses rugged high country for a few miles, revealing views of the redrock country far into Utah. I remember it as a seemingly impenetrable maze of rocks, where one might easily become lost, never to be found again. From the high country the trail takes switchback turns down into deep, colorful canyons so narrow that in places one cannot glimpse the sky above.

Near the day's end, we reached our campsite in an echoing sandstone amphitheater, perhaps half a mile above the bridge. I tarried only a few minutes, the magnetic lure of the bridge overcame weariness, and I soon glimpsed it for the first time. In the shadows of evening solitude, it was awe-inspiring. That night I slept little. The combination of excitement and a constant chorus of frogs vibrating their vocal pouches, the sound amplified by the acoustical effect of the overhanging sandstone, shell-like cave, was too much.

Next day was beautiful, and after taking pictures to my heart's content, I lolled in a long, clear-water pool beneath the bridge, while my two companions went on down to the Colorado River. A day of impressions I'll never forget. I've been up to Rainbow in a boat several times since, but much of its attractiveness has been lost for me because of easy access and crowds of people. However, it will still be a great thrill for all who view it for the first time, even under present conditions. Let's all hope it will not become another victim of man's "progress."

I've not had the thrill of running the Colorado River by boat either above Lake Powell or through the Grand Canyon but I have tasted a bit of river running. Mira and I have run the Rogue and the Owyhee in Oregon. Both are considered to be among the wildest and most beautiful of western rivers. We also experienced the adventure of a boat trip down the Yampa River in Colorado and the Green River in Utah through Dinosaur National Monument. That trip is one to remember — the silence of the deep, narrow canyon of the Yampa, where the stream glides smoothly until the roar of rapids ahead becomes audible. The excitement of running the rapids of these rivers provides thrills aplenty. Occasionally deer, beaver, and other wild animals are caught unaware as the boat glides along making no sound. Once I flushed three deer when I went ashore for pictures. They leaped over a 10-foot cliff into the stream where there was no place to go but with the swift current. We finally caught them, exhausted, standing in shallows on a sagebrush-covered peninsula, too tired to go further or worry about our close proximity. There was no escape for them except downstream. The river fills the bottom of the deep canyon from wall to wall for miles with only an occasional point of land interrupting its racing descent. The current is too swift to swim upstream. We left them in their new, temporary home as we moved on down toward the confluence with the Green River many miles away at Echo Park, a beautiful and spectacular area of cottonwood groves, flat parkland, and towering canyon walls which can be reached by road. Our night camps were serenaded by angry slaps of beaver tails on the water, expressing their indignation for our intrusion into their remote domain.

Zion, Bryce, and Cedar Breaks have been subjects for my camera many times since my first trip west introduced me to the attractions of the southwest Utah wonderland.

My most memorable Bryce visit was one of a couple of winter trips to that colorful spot. It is never more beautiful than it is following a snowstorm. I had a field day that finished with me in a state of exhaustion after I had skied into the depths of the amphitheater. One exhilarating run on perfect snow was not quite so perfect because of the climb back out to the rim. The thin layer of new snow on the crust beneath was great during the comparative weightlessness of the descent, but each climbing step broke through the too-thin crust into deep powder beneath. It was dark when I finally reached the 8,000-foot rim.

My ski pictures had brought invitations to visit several winter resorts of the West, and for that matter, an offer from the Swiss National Tourist Bureau to visit Switzerland, cost-free. The latter I decided not to accept because I felt that two months away from my home grounds in the West was more than my budding business would bear. But I did spend a week or so each winter at such places as Alta, Utah; Sun Valley, Idaho; and later, in the 50s and early 60s at Squaw Valley, and Sugar Bowl in California. When weather was not ideal for pictures, I enjoyed some grand skiing. Photos I took on assignment at Squaw Valley were instrumental in that resort being awarded the 1960 Winter Olympics. Those winter trips were not without incident nor without accident. More things happened to me than to anyone I know of, but I'll not bore the reader with those episodes here.

The Southwest abounds with areas and individual subjects that have left outstanding impressions in my memories. A great deal depends on conditions that exist at the time one first sees a place or when he sees it for the hundredth time. The Grand Canyon, for instance, can be comparatively unimpressive viewed under normal lighting or weather conditions. The serious, seasoned photographer, whether amateur or professional, who is familiar with the Grand Canyon, knows that it is usually at its magnificent best shortly before sunset or just after sunrise. Add thunderstorms or fresh winter snow and the Canyon will drive you out of your mind. Those thunderstorms are most frequent during summer afternoons when the average traveler makes it a point to shy away from the Southwest because of the well-known desert heat. But the average traveler doesn't know that the 8,000-foot altitude of the Grand Canyon tempers that heat tremendously.

Seasons, too, have more effect on the attractions of some areas than others. Death Valley in winter or spring can be great. Its heat is unbearable in summer. The highlands of Colorado, Utah, and New Mexico offer something different for almost any season, but I have been most impressed with those regions in the fall when autumn colors add another dimension to the already impressive spectacle of towering mountains. Most of Colorado's mountain region has more than its share of autumn color, but there is an area in southwestern Colorado which includes the San Juan and San Miguel ranges that is just fantastically beautiful in the fall. Each autumn season is different than the preceding

one. Add to those ranges the Dolores River, and other areas to the east, and the photographer has a studio full of nature's beauty at its best.

The lower desert regions of New Mexico, Arizona, Nevada, and California usually are at their best with the floral beauty of springtime. Sometimes rainfall may not be sufficient or timely to produce a profusion of flowers, such as poppies and verbena. It is a rare and thrilling occasion that should be fully enjoyed when the lower desert region is ablaze with floral color. Unlike those plants that spread their blossoms in profusion over the sandy wastes, cactus blooms are more scattered and vary in color as well as in the timing of their dress parade. Few blossoms of any type equal the beauty of some species of cacti.

Nevada always impresses me with its deceptive distances of sagebrush rangeland. Mountain range after mountain range beckon travelers in all directions, appearing to be within easy reach, but the distance is always far greater than the eye can estimate.

California is so large and varied, it is even more difficult to decide on a selected number of highlights to represent this state. The protected bristle cone pine region on the high, windswept crest of the White Mountains is impossible to describe or understand. Here, in clusters and standing alone, the magnificent trees have withstood the ravages of time and the most violent climatic conditions for thousands of years. Here are the oldest living things on this earth. Far below stretches the Owens Valley with a hundred-mile expanse of the eastern escarpment of the high, rugged Sierra Nevada Range scraping the sky in the background, creating a panorama equaled in few other places I know of.

The wilderness areas in the Sierras, too few of which I have seen, are havens of semi-solitude for California's multitudes of outdoor enthusiasts. Yosemite National Park is a far cry from wilderness classification. This fantastically beautiful park can be most appreciated during the spring and autumn seasons when less crowded and when waterfalls and autumn foliage add to the natural beauty.

By now, the reader must be aware that I am more interested in nature than the works of man. The spectacles of the great cities can best be left for other volumes.

It is impossible to ignore the California Coast and its outstanding beauty, too little of which can still be enjoyed by the public. Some success has been achieved in improving the California Coast situation with some fine state parks as well as a couple of national parks.

Numerous endowed redwood groves and Redwood National Park reveal a bit of the great redwood forests which are being preserved for present and future generations. Visitors to the redwood region must stray from the freeway and main traveled highways into some of these magnificent groves to fully appreciate them.

Mt. Lassen, Mt. Shasta, Burney Falls, and the rugged Trinity Alps in extreme northern California are of great interest. Shasta, second highest of the volcanic peaks in the Cascade Range, dominates the region despite surrounding civilization and its all too evident effect which detracts from the surrounding environment.

I've been most impressed with Tule Lake Wildlife Refuge during frequent autumn visits when millions of waterfowl, and I do mean millions, rendezvous for rest and feeding during their migratory journey from the northland of Canada to their winter home in the warm valleys of central California. It's an exciting experience to be on hand when the evening flight of these birds takes place, and watching as incredible numbers of them take to the air during a half-hour period of time. One cloudy evening about sunset, I was sitting on the edge of one of the dikes awaiting the usual evening spectacle. The overcast had left too little light for color pictures. Suddenly a sonic boom from a high flying military jet created an experience I'll never forget. The millions of geese and ducks burst from their resting places in one giant explosion. The tumult of their cries and desperate flight lasted for several minutes. I was really glad the cameras were packed away so that I was permitted an undistracted impression of this unique experience.

Delicate Arch clings precariously to the edge of a wind-sculptured sandstone bowl in Arches National Park, Utah. A large number of arches and windows can be found in the park.

Superstition Mountain in cactus land of central Arizona played an important historical role in the early-day life of the state. To this day prospectors search its rugged slopes for lost gold mines.

Clear water of Oak Creek pours over colorful stone of Oak Creek Canyon, a favorite playground and retirement home region of central Arizona.

Alta, Utah, is located in a steep walled canyon rich in mining lore of bygone days. Alta has for years been regarded as one of the world's finest ski areas by those who prefer deep, dry powder snow common to the Wasatch Range.

Bryce Canyon National Park, Utah, is probably the most colorful area in this vast, fantastic region. Winter snow enhances the beauty of this amphitheater by reflecting light into shadowed areas. In turn, the colors of surrounding cliffs and spires are reflected in pastel tints on the surface of the snow.

The Grand Canyon is never more spectacular than when illuminated by late afternoon sunlight during or after frequent summer thunderstorms. Under such conditions cliffs and rock formations stand out in bold relief against shifting cloud shadows.

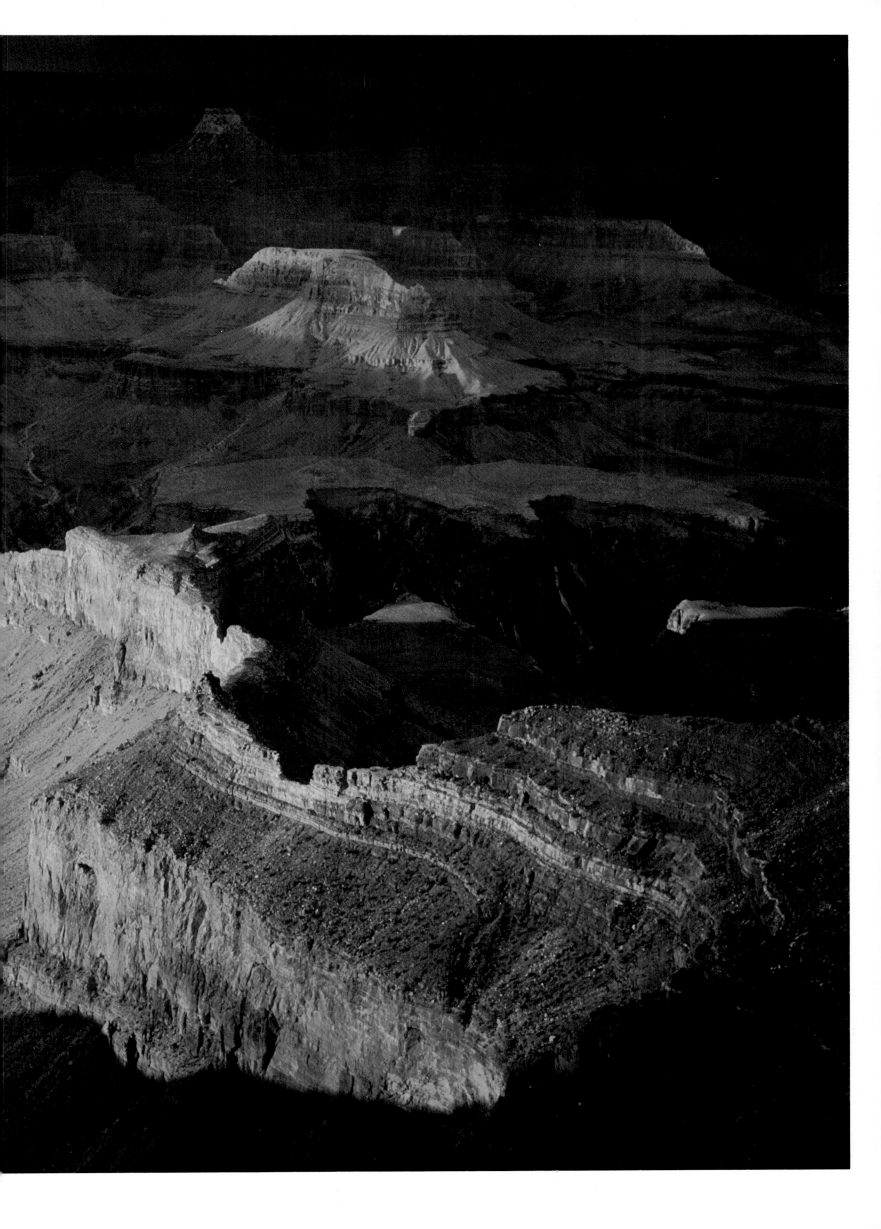

Controversial Lake Powell created by Glen Canyon Dam on the Colorado River in Arizona has numerous tributaries like Labyrinth Canyon, which can be explored by boat.

Lake Powell viewed from the air conveys most effectively the unique character of this controversial creation of man. The bed of the Colorado River lies under hundreds of feet of water. The river's eighteen-hundred-mile shoreline reaches back into mysteriously beautiful canyons and desert valleys.

Rainbow Bridge National Monument, Utah, is one of the wonders of the world. Until creation of Lake Powell by Glen Canyon Dam on the Colorado River made Rainbow accessible by boat, it was reached after many miles of travel along the fabulous Rainbow trail pictured on the opposite page. The bridge is so large it could span the dome of the U. S. Capitol building. Now it is in danger of destruction by undermining effects of the lake water.

The Canyon of the Escalante River is almost filled for many miles by waters of Lake Powell. It is one of the more popular of many tributary canyons for exploration by boaters.

The San Juan River has carved a tortuous route through the redrock country of southeastern Utah.
Water of Lake Powell reaches for many miles up the San Juan Canyon.

Canyonlands National Park, formerly penetrated only by foot or horseback, has succumbed to off-road motor vehicle travel. However some areas, such as Chesler Park, featured in this picture, have been closed to vehicle access to prevent erosion of approach routes.

Grand Falls of the Little Colorado River, normally dry, is most spectacular during springtime melt of snow water in the distant mountains and following thunderstorms of cloudburst proportions.

Bryce Canyon National Park in southern Utah. Actually the park is a series of amphitheaters where the high plateau rim breaks off into lower country. These amphitheaters include a maze of canyons, spires, and ridges, colorful beyond description. Winter snow adds to the spectacular beauty by reflecting light into shadowed coves; in turn tints of color are reflected on the surface of the snow.

Cedar Breaks National Monument is a condensed amphitheater similar to several in Bryce Canyon National Park. Shades of color are perhaps more delicate. Only a small area of the Breaks is included in this view across a grove of golden autumn-colored aspen.

The upper reaches of the Escalante River, Utah, where the stream runs free, photographed in the rosy glow of the setting sun.

A heavy autumn snowstorm blankets Dallas Divide in southwestern Colorado before ranchers had moved their cattle to the lowlands. The peak of Mt. Sneffels, one of Colorado's many mountains over 14,000 feet high, dominates the background skyline.

Autumn glory in aspen groves and forests of oak cover the foothills of the San Juan Range at the foot of Mt. Sneffels.

Golden aspen foliage frames a vista of Wilson Peak in southwestern Colorado in the San Miguel Range. Wilson Peak and Mt. Wilson are over 14,000 feet high.

The San Juan Range in southwestern Colorado provides an impressive panorama viewed from near Ridgeway just after an autumn snow-storm has decorated the lofty range.

A beautiful blending of new snow and autumn-tinted aspen foliage in the San Miguel Range in southwestern Colorado.

Death Valley National Monument in southeastern California has many attractions that make the area a popular winter resort and tourist attraction. Travel is discouraged during summer months when desert heat is almost unbearable. Among the most familiar and picturesque attractions are the mesquite flats sand dunes near Stove Pipe Wells.

The Merced River makes a spectacular leap over granite cliffs of Yosemite National Park, California, at Nevada Falls. A fine, much traveled trail reaches the falls and beyond.

Joshua Tree National Monument in the Little San Bernardino Mountains of Southern California is a weird land of grotesque Joshua trees, cactus, and other desert vegetation surrounding fantastic rock formations that reach high above the desert.

Pacific surf lashes the southern California shoreline at La Jolla.

Winter snow contrasts with Ponderosa Pine trees on the Nevada shore of Lake Tahoe. The distant mountains rise above the California shore. The state line divides Tahoe almost equally for the two states.

Historic Donner Lake from Donner Pass. Here the ill-fated Donner Party of pioneers spent a tragic winter unable to cross the pass because of deep snow. Now motorists speed across the Sierras at Donner on a modern freeway. Between fifty and a hundred thousand skiers visit the general area each weekend and thousands of them keep several modern winter playgrounds like Squaw Valley, pictured on Page 65, busy every day of the winter season.

Shore birds search busily for food as the Pacific surf rolls up on the sands of the Monterey Peninsula at sunset.

Pacific tides wash and wear the rocks into intricate patterns along the shoreline at Point Lobos Reserve State Park below Carmel Highlands.

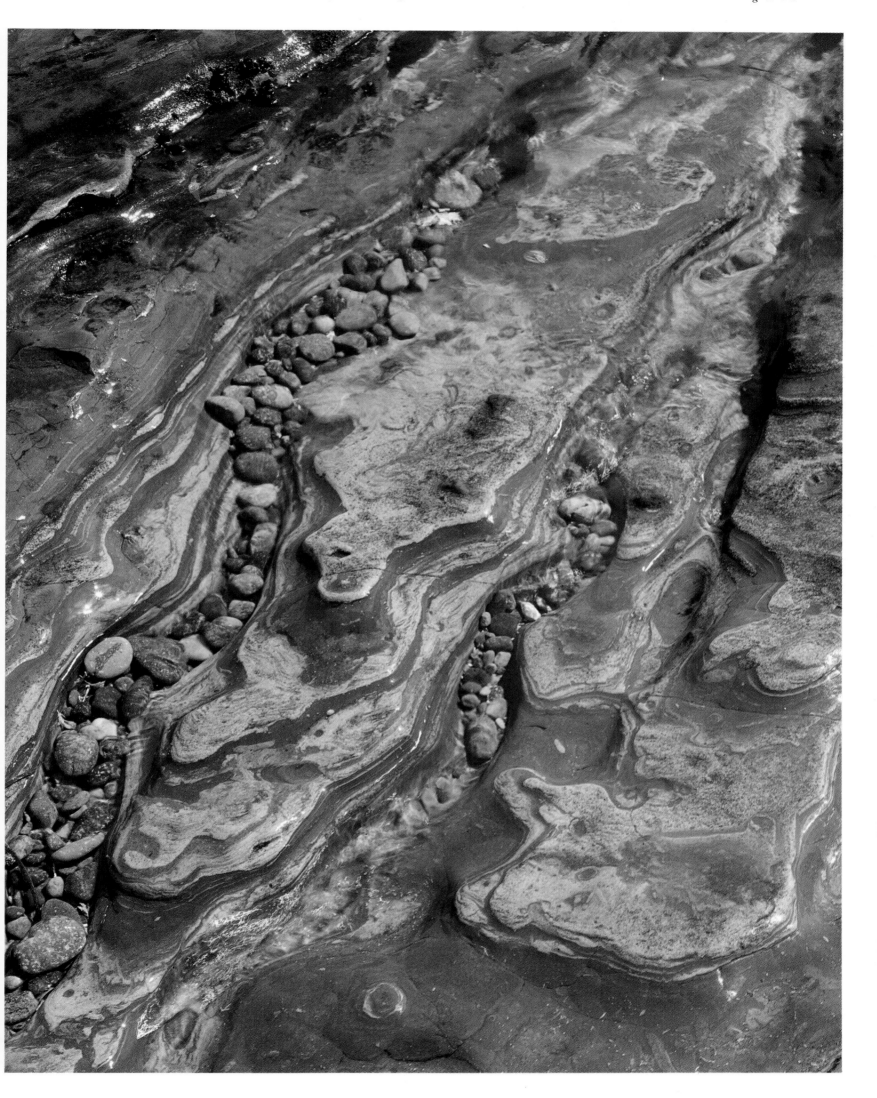

Owen Valley nestled between the Sierra Nevada Range and the White Mountains in eastern California is a colorfully decorated stage for the autumn foliage show. Here livestock roam the range and recreationists consider the Owen Valley the gateway to high mountain adventure.

Bristle cone pine trees, said to be the oldest living things on earth, have battled winds, snow and rain for thousands of years on the otherwise barren, open crest of the White Mountains at an elevation of 12,000 feet where this photo was taken.

Thousand Island Lake is a favorite rendezvous for hikers and campers in Minarets Wilderness. It lies at an elevation of ten thousand feet at the foot of Banner and Ritter Peaks in the Sierra Nevada Range.

Blossoms of shooting star, also popularly known as bird bill, sway in the mountain breeze beside a stream in Minarets Wilderness in the Sierra Nevada Range.

Rhododendrons bloom in profusion in fog-shrouded Redwood National Park along the north-western coastal region of California.

Kayakers race down swift rapids of the Feather River in northern California. The Feather is not always like this because its waters are harnessed by dams which control the flow of the stream.

Cold, clear water of Kings River flows swiftly over its boulder-strewn course in Kings Canyon National Park in the Sierra Nevada Range.

Oranges are most synonymous with California even though other agricultural crops such as grapes, tomatoes, lettuce, etc. have outstripped the production of oranges in the rich agricultural valleys of the state.

California's dairyland in the rolling hills of Marin and Sonoma counties is especially attractive in its springtime dress of velvety green pasture grass.

McArthur-Burney Falls State Park is highlighted by the unique character of the falls. Here the main stream pouring over a high lava cliff in twin falls joined by countless springs which gush from the walls in a veil of beauty.

Mt. Shasta in northern California is the second highest peak in the Cascade Range. Its 14,162-foot volcanic crest looks down on Shastina, a second peak 12,000 feet in height. The two peaks combine to make one massive mountain that sometimes creates its own weather as moisture-laden atmosphere flowing inland from the Pacific condenses into clouds over the lofty crest of the mountain.

The Northwest

Where is the Northwest? The word and the concept have been interpreted variously in different places and in different times. Residents of the eastern states may think of it as beginning somewhere around Minnesota and stretching to the Pacific. People who live in areas of the Far West are inclined to be more exclusive in their idea of the Northwest.

The Minnesota conception probably is left over from earlier days, when anything west of the Mississippi was referred to as the Northwest. Little was known of the vast land farther west.

In the Preface, I said that my impressions of the West would not be geographically bound, and other than mentioning various states and specific places, I have really avoided geographical boundaries. I've even strayed as far West as the Hawaiian Islands, which logically would be identified with the Southwest. But because my many visits to the Islands originated from my home in Portland, the Northwest section of text will include some of my most memorable impressions of the 50th state.

My first Island visit was in 1951, long before Hawaii became a state. The main islands were at that time far different in character and aspect than they are now. They projected a feeling that perhaps few of the more recent residents and visitors can comprehend. A few good hotels on Oahu and two to four on the "Outer Islands" accommodated visitors. A high percentage of the population were native Hawaiians, though even then Hawaii was sometimes referred to as "a melting pot."

I had the good fortune to receive a three-week assignment to photograph Hawaii and some of its people for United Air Lines. Afterward, I lingered another three weeks to revisit certain areas like Hana (Maui), Kona (Hawaii), Kauai, and, of course, Oahu. During my assignment, I found that the sun didn't always shine in that Pacific Paradise when and where I wanted it. After a succession of visits I gradually acquired a knowledge of Island weather that helped me to time my rambles to take full advantage of optimum conditions.

One of my later trips was as a tour conductor for "Through the Lens Tours." The most pleasing aspect of that trip was that Mira accompanied me and enjoyed the Islands for the first time. An extra treat that time was the spectacle of a volcanic eruption.

Certain areas would make a strong impression on my mind as I made return trips. I recall swimming in Warm Springs on a couple of occasions before a major volcanic eruption buried it beneath a deep lava flow; photographing the surf action during several visits to picturesque Opihikao; the fern forest, White Sands Beach, a ride along the Kona Coast in an outboard canoe with a native spear fisherman while porpoises swam alongside, close enough to be touched from the boat. Mira and I thrilled to a helicopter ride along the Na Pali Coast, and up the Kalalau Valley when copter flight service was just beginning. The pilot left us on a remote beach for several hours, picking us up later at a point back along the trail.

The highlight of our trips to Haena and the Na Pali area were days on a lovely beach, picking up beautiful shells. That was before the area became populated with young transients from the mainland. On two different occasions, we were treated to spectacular surf action at the Na Pali Cliffs, probably our most thrilling impression of the Islands.

When I was actively covering assignments in the late forties and fifties, I learned that many eastern publishers and the editors of most national publications that originated in the East had the strange impression that Montana and Wyoming were as accessible from Portland as perhaps Massachusetts or Pennsylvania from New York, and that British Columbia was just close by. I covered numerous British Columbia assignments for Saturday Evening Post, Holiday, National Geographic, etc., and frequently was called upon to rush over, upon a moment's notice, to some remote Montana and Idaho location in addition to covering Oregon and Washington stories. Most of these assignments had tight deadlines and it was extremely difficult to manage complicated travel situations, sometimes involving various milk-run plane schedules or long trips by car, all of which helped to familiarize me with the Northwest, but permitted little or no opportunity to capture a few pictures for my own stock file.

Actually, the trips Mira and I had made earlier, in the 30s, though shorter with one exception, were the ones I enjoyed most and were most productive of pictures. That one exception was a 1933 autumn trip in my old '29 Ford back "home" to visit my mother, brothers, and sister, as well as friends. It was a grand trip. I had fitted up the car so we could sleep in it, and we did a considerable amount of exploring, including our first visit to Yellowstone, the Tetons, and the Black Hills, enroute to my brother's home in Milwaukee.

One other experience of the 30s served to familiarize the State of Washington to Mira and me. We spent most of one summer in the early 30s traveling in my old Model A to all the C.C.C. camps where I photographed camps and personnel. Between camps, I managed to accumulate quite a few black and white photos for my growing file of pictures, and some for the studio.

Our weekend explorations were lengthened, at times, to include Saturday afternoons, so we managed to stray farther from home, climbing more mountains, hiking new trails, and taking an occasional trip to more distant coastal areas.

The glaciers of Mt. Hood, Mt. Adams, and Mt. St. Helens, as well as their summits, became our part-time playground and studio. Mira made most of these hikes and climbs with our small group, as well as ski trips, which usually involved night climbs to a new cabin our Wy'east Club had built near Timberline on Mt. Hood. My only ascent of Mt. Rainier was made with two other Wy'easters on a clear day, but the wind was terrifically strong on the summit dome, stinging our faces with ice pellets and, at times, blowing us from our footing. Of more than eighty climbers on the mountain that weekend, we alone reached the summit, where my dark glasses were blown away. As we descended, we found that one large party was in trouble. One unroped climber had been dislodged by the wind and had slid back down the slope. He was later found dead in a crevasse. We made several descents and ascents of the Gibraltar Chute aiding members of the party down the mountain, and when we finally started for home, I was forced to turn over the driving to a companion because my eyes had passed their limit of exposure to the snow-reflected sunlight.

About 1937, when the first Kodachrome film became available, Mira, our small daughter Eleanor, another couple, and I enjoyed a grand vacation trip to southern Utah's colorful wonderland, the north rim of the Grand Canyon, and across Death Valley and the Sierras to the California Coast before returning home. A lot of color film rolled through my little Bantam special camera (I still have the camera), especially in the more colorful area of Utah. But, sad to relate, all the color film became pale and worthless in a couple of years' time. The only durable pictures left from that trip are some I took of the San Francisco Fair on Treasure Island, apparently taken on improved film.

Back again now to my later freelance days which began in 1946. There were opportunities to take Mira and Eleanor along as I phased away from assignment work. Glacier National Park, Montana's most photogenic and exciting region, was explored several times. Yellowstone and the Tetons we revisited time after time. Those were the uncrowded days, some of them in autumn, usually the most colorful and least crowded season. I remember a trip across Bear Tooth Pass between Cook and Deer Lodge, Montana, when the evening light whetted my photographic appetite. Spectacular mountain scenery highlighted by golden, autumn-tinted aspen groves tempted me to camp overnight. Instead I drove on to Deer Lodge for the night with intentions of returning next morning. It's fortunate I made that decision. A terrific blizzard that night closed the Pass for the season, so I headed northward hoping for a break in the storm. It was tough going. I reached St. Mary's Junction at Glacier Park by nightfall in deep snow. Next day I spent scouting picture settings, took half a dozen shots during brief sunlight breaks and lay awake till well after midnight planning for a great day of shooting — the sky had completely cleared after dark. Sometime before I went to sleep, a high wind came up and I knew another trip had been blown. No snow nor autumn foliage was left on the trees, so I headed homeward.

Many, many frustrations in various guises have been my lot. Mira frequently said I could write a book about those frustrations and narrow escapes of one type or another. One location I discovered while scouting around in southern Montana was so impressive I made three journeys in as many years before I finally was on the scene when conditions were favorable.

I was invited to photograph Yellowstone highlights in winter, travel to be by snow plane — a plane-like vehicle combining engine, propeller, and large ski runners — an innovation at the time. I drove the thousand miles on three different winters before conditions favored us. On the third try we enjoyed a couple of beautiful picture days at the geysers and Yellowstone Lake. Old Faithful cooperated, and I skied across a mile or so to try for some shots of buffalo browsing through the snow. For awhile they cooperated but when they decided I shouldn't bother them any more, I suddenly found myself helplessly frozen to the spot. The cold surface snow was deceptive; the snow underneath had been turned to adhesive consistency by the geyser-warmed ground. I couldn't move out of my tracks until both skis were removed. Then I beat a quick retreat, wading in the deep snow with rucksack and skis over my shoulders.

The Devil's Tower in eastern Wyoming with a prairie dog village nearby once provided an interesting afternoon for Mira, Eleanor, and me, and we've enjoyed the spectacular Needles and Rushmore Monument in the Black Hills.

Idaho's Sawtooth Range and Stanley Basin have lured me a few times, and I've spent many weeks of many winters at Sun Valley. An autumn view of Payette Lake fringed with golden larch, seen from a vantage point high above the Eastern shore, was an outstanding sight among many such visual treats offered by the Idaho lakes.

One morning I got out early — too early, it proved to be — to photograph sunrise tints on the Sawtooth Range from the outlet of Redfish Lake, the headwaters of the Salmon River. As I shivered in the predawn chill, I heard a splashing in the river. Investigating, I discovered three otters at play. A large pine tree had toppled at a steep angle into the river, and the otters were romping up a large limb to a high point on the tree and sliding about 30 feet down the tree trunk, worn smooth, wet, and slippery by long use. Suddenly one dove from the trunk about 15 feet into the river and came up with a salmon as large as the otter, and wildly flapping. Away it went into the lake with the other two in hot pursuit. Oh, for some light to have captured some of that action on film.

Of course, Oregon and Washington are most familiar to me, having been my principal outdoor studio for 45 years; so familiar that highlight impressions are almost impossible to pick out. The Olympic Rain Forest is a separate world. Volcanic peaks of the Cascades in both states are so similar as to make it difficult to choose a favorite, yet so different when one has the opportunity to explore their slopes and immediate surroundings that a choice becomes even more difficult. The rivers and especially the smaller, moss-bowered streams and falls will never become commonplace despite their numbers.

The mighty Columbia River, so greatly altered in character by the mammoth dams along its length, flows through regions as varied as one can imagine.

Visitors unfamiliar with the Pacific Northwest usually are surprised to learn that these two states have characteristics of climate and geology far different than those associated with the towering, glacier-clad, volcanic cones, evergreen forests, and rugged Pacific coastline.

Two-thirds of Oregon is east of the Cascade Range. It is high desert country broken here and there by other mountain ranges, such as the Wallowas, Blue Mountains, and Steens. Similar desert-like regions of Eastern Washington have been changed by vast reclamation projects into rich agricultural land as extensive as some eastern states. The Cascade Range acts as a barrier, wringing moisture from Pacific storms, leaving comparatively little for the semi-arid, sagebrush land east of the range.

Even the Olympic Range in northwestern Washington is a barrier that creates a remarkable change in climatic conditions within a 30- or 40-mile airline distance. The 12-foot annual rainfall of the Olympic Rain Forest nestled between the seashore and the mountains becomes a mere 17 inches in the flat land between Puget Sound and the eastern foothills of the Olympics.

Crater Lake, Oregon's only National Park, is something else again. It, like the Grand Canyon, and other outstanding scenic attractions, changes its character under varied lighting and weather conditions. My first brief midday visit to the rim of the lake left me disappointed and unimpressed. Since then I've seen it in many moods, some of them indescribably beautiful. A hike down the trail for an early morning boat ride on the deep blue, mirror surface of the lake is an experience never forgotten. Usually that ethereal effect is lost later in the day when the water ripples in the wind.

Oregon boasts perhaps the greatest number and variety of state parks in the country. Farsighted officials like Governor West and nature-lover Sam Boardman left their marks on the State of Oregon with their diligent acquisition and development of state parks when land was more available than it is now. The system has expanded under other leadership in the ensuing years.

A few years ago I was in the thick of a battle to acquire Cape Kiwanda for park supervision. Kiwanda is a spot I consider to be the most photogenic anywhere on the American coast, east or west. Top state officials had frequently indicated they favored the acquisition of Kiwanda and were working toward that goal. They were quoted as stating that "the State should acquire and protect Kiwanda to preserve its wild beauty." Finally the Cape was acquired, and the ink on acquisition papers had hardly dried when a very costly and unsightly wire-mesh fence, indiscriminately located across much of that "wild beauty" that was to be preserved, was erected. The visitors who climbed up the Cape were halted in a fenced-in pen, preventing access to points where the once beautiful Cape would be viewed to best advantage. The most hazardous point that supposedly was the reason for the fence is directly accessible because drifting sand there keeps the barrier covered. Changes were promised, but at this writing, the beauty of Cape Kiwanda is still a casualty of inconceivably poor planning. Any area of outstanding beauty worthy of state park status certainly deserves more considerate treatment.

I hope that the natural treasures which are the rivers, forests, coastline, desert, and mountains of the West will be treated with more thoughtful consideration in the years ahead.

A freshwater spring pours from a moss-covered cliff in Oregon's Cascade Range. Constant spray from the splashing water nourishes the growth of abundant moss.

Deep winter snow on Mt. Hood's lofty volcanic cone seems to ignore the springtime aspect of the Hood River Valley orchard and pastureland far below.

Visitors to Crater Lake National Park may receive the ultimate thrill of their visit if afforded the opportunity to hike the trail to the shore for an early morning boat trip around the lake when the water's surface is most apt to be calm.

Crater Lake after a midwinter snowstorm is a sight not soon forgotten. The highway is kept open for travel to the rim all through the winter.

Turbulent Pacific surf lashes offshore rocks as it vents its angry mood during stormy weather along the Oregon Coast.

Northwest mountains receive more than their share of snowfall during the winter season. As a result,
numerous winter playgrounds lure skiers to settings such as this at Anthony Lakes on the crest of Oregon's
Blue Mountain Range.

(Overleaf) Glorious sunset colors reflected from clouds silhouette The Needles, which have withstood
thousands of years of pounding by the Pacific surf at Cannon Beach, Oregon.

The alpine glow of a winter sunset adds to the illusion of unreality in this fantasy scene of storm-sculptured creatures on timberline trees on the slope of Mt. Hood, Oregon.

The McKenzie River gets off to a roaring start just a half mile below its source in Oregon's Cascade range. Here it leaps over a forest-bound cliff at Sahalie Falls.

The symmetrical cone of Mt. Hood is silhouetted by the ruby glow of sunrise reflected on moody clouds as lights of suburban Portland still twinkle in the Willamette Valley below.

Oneonta Gorge is a spectacular fracture in lava walls of the Columbia River Gorge where Oneonta Creek has found its way to its confluence with the Columbia.

In the land of Christmas trees in Oregon's Cascade Range fir trees are decorated with a new blanket of ermine after a winter storm.

Wherever sunlight can penetrate the dense evergreen forests of Oregon and Washington vine maple foliage glows in brillant hues.

The early bird gets the fish seems to be the theory here on Tillamook Bay, Oregon,
where salmon fishermen are busy trolling as the rising sun clothes fog and water in colorful beauty.

A sports fishing boat leaps across the Pacific surf as it leaves the beach at Cape Kiwanda heading for deep sea salmon fishing around Haystack Rock a mile off shore.

Fog creates a mystic atmosphere as it penetrates a forest in Cape Lookout State Park where fern and other plant life covers the forest floor.

Pacific fog rolls up the mountain slopes into a picturesque forest at Cape Mears State Park on the Oregon Coast.

*Intricate patterns are revealed by the reflected sunset glow where
a creek spreads out across the sand to meet the Pacific surf at
Beverly Beach State Park on the Oregon Coast.*

Wild geese in flight at Oregon's Malheur National Wildlife Refuge are silhouetted by tumbling thunderheads. Many Wildlife refuges are located throughout the west.

A beautiful sunset is a thrilling spectacle wherever it may occur. There is little to choose between these two. One silhouetting Mt. McLoughlin and the Cascade Range viewed across the tranquil surface of Klamath Lake in Southern Oregon is perhaps more serene than the setting on the Oregon Coast where Twin Rocks tower above the turbulent surf.

Mt. Hood's volcanic cone presents different characteristics when viewed from various vantage points. Framed by weathered trees on the crest of Larch Mountain the gleaming white peak dominates the distant skyline as ominous clouds threaten its serene mood.

Club moss draped over a maple tree is mute testimony to the abundant moisture that drenches the famed Olympic Rain Forest in Olympic National Park, Washington.

Wild rhododendron grow and bloom in profusion in many areas from the redwood forests of northern California through western Oregon and western Washington. It is the state flower of Washington.

A salmon leaps a rapids of a tributary stream of the Columbia as it fights its way to its birthplace to spawn and die after spending several migratory years at sea.

The Cascade Range might well have received its name because of thousands of cascading streams that rush down the slopes of the mountains. Oregon pioneers were especially impressed by one cascade, which was an obstacle to conquer on their journey down the Columbia River through that mountain range. The cascades of the Columbia River now lie buried beneath backwater above Bonneville Dam in the Columbia Gorge. The range was named for the Cascades.

Blue and gold clouds on the horizon reflect the brilliant glow of sunset while the dark surf of the Pacific rolls toward the Washington coastline.

Mt. Rainier, "Monarch of the Northwest" at 14,410 feet, is the highest peak in the Cascade Range. It is the heart of Mt. Rainier National Park. The majestic, glacier-clad mountain is surrounded by numerous alpine meadows sprinkled with wild flowers in late summer. The photo was taken from a slope on the Tatoosh Range.

The Austin Pass Shelter at the foot of Table Mountain in Mt. Baker National Forest in Washington's North Cascade Range might resemble the imaginary home of St. Nicholas. This is a popular winter and summer recreation area.

Mt. Shuksan probably lures more visitors for its autumn dress parade than does any other Northwest area. The kaleidoscope of huckleberry, blueberry, and mountain ash spread out among picturesque evergreen trees at the foot of the rugged mountain attracts thousands of people from nearby Puget Sound cities as well as residents of Vancouver, British Columbia, just across the Canadian border.

Vine maple foliage mingled with giant evergreens overlooking Swift Reservoir in southern Washington creates a colorful setting beneath autumn sunlight.

Steam rising from comparatively warm waters of Wood River deposits a frosty icing on trees and shrubs on a frigid morning in Sun Valley, Idaho.

Lake Pend Oreille (pronounced Ponderay) in northern Idaho is justly famed for its beauty, tremendous size, and extreme depth, as well as for the huge trout that are caught from its waters.

Jagged crags in the Sawtooth Range of Idaho tower high above Redfish Creek where a fisherman whips the riffles with his line.

Sun Valley, Idaho, is probably the most famous western winter playground. Skiers travel from all over the world to enjoy its superlative snow conditions and ski runs like this one on Baldy Mountain.

A frosty autumn morning decorates the tip of evergreen trees with candles of ice in the Lochsaw River Canyon of Idaho.

Mists rise into the mountains from the Lochsaw
River on a nippy autumn morning. Lewis and
Clark crossed Lolo Pass from Montana down into
the Lochsaw, then turned away from the narrow,
rugged canyon to cross over the top of the
Bitterroot Range. Chief Joseph also led his
people in their retreat across much the same route.

Autumn sunshine sparkles on the rippling waters of the Snake River in Swan Valley, Idaho, where cottonwood and aspen trees glow in golden beauty.

A fisherman lands another big trout from swift-flowing waters of the Galatin River in southern Montana near Bozeman.

Cottonwood trees still decorated with the golden foliage of autumn receive a surprise visit from early-arriving winter weather which almost overwhelms the smaller trees with a heavy blanket of snow in northern Montana.

An early snowstorm is unsuccessful in obliterating the beauty of autumn foliage beside Lower St. Mary Lake in Montana. It only succeeds in enhancing the magnificent scene.

*The Yellowstone River curves gracefully through farm and
rangeland of aptly named Paradise Valley at the foot of the Absaroka
Range of mountains in southern Montana.*

A rainbow in the spray at the foot of Yellowstone Falls almost steals the show from the falls and the cliffs over which the river plunges.

The colorful glow of a frigid winter sunrise paints the lofty Teton Range while frost still clings to shrubs and trees in early morning shadows of Jackson Hole, Wyoming.

Green River Lakes mirror Square Top Mountain and other peaks of the Wind River Range as evening shadows shroud the lake shore.

Old Faithful puts on its hourly show even for a small audience, as snow plane drivers enjoy the spectacle on a calm, winter day.

A fringe of golden autumn-tinted cottonwood trees contrast beautifully with the blue waters of the Snake River as it prepares to leave Wyoming's Jackson Hole enroute westward to Idaho.

The Devil's Tower is a magnetic lure from wherever it may be seen. It is the heart of a national monument in the rolling rangeland region of eastern Wyoming. It has been scaled by several adventurous mountaineers.

Random Impressions

Although Mt. Olympus in Olympic National Park, Washington, is only 7,985 feet in elevation, precipitation is so great that the mountain is draped with several huge glaciers that pour down its slopes to a very low altitude. The Blue Glacier dominates this scene.

A picturesque wind-sculptured pine tree has gained a solid toehold on a wind-eroded pedestal and apparently intends to stay there in colorful Zion National Park in Southern Utah.

Squaw Grass, as it is known in Oregon, is also called Bear Grass and Indian Basket Grass in other western regions where it grows prolifically. Its cream-colored blooms are erratic in their habits. Some years they cover their habitat so abundantly as to resemble snowfields viewed from a distance: another year hardly a bloom may be found.

The Snake River flows in artistic curves through rangeland of Jackson Hole, Wyoming, just before entering a deep, rugged canyon that rushes its waters westward toward Idaho.

The scalloped dome of one of the large rooms of
Mt. Rainier's Paradise Ice Caves is illuminated in
translucent beauty as sunlight filters through the
comparatively thin ice. The caverns, created by
warmer currents of air from swift flowing streams
beneath the glacier, sometimes collapse and new
caverns are formed at a different location. Some
years after an excessive snowfall the caves may
not be accessible to visitors.

Late afternoon sunlight and shadows play across the ridges and canyons of Grand Canyon National Park. Under such conditions the Park visitor is treated to an indescribably exciting show of nature and beauty.

*Josephine Lake mirrors precipitous mountain beauty of Glacier National Park during the tranquil,
early morning hours just after sunrise.*

Cathedral Gorge in Nevada lives up to half its name with its fluted spires and mysterious, narrow passages into the heart of weathered formations. Its classification as a gorge is, however, a bit mystifying.

Tiger lily seems to be a misnomer for this delicately beautiful flower common to the Northwest. Perhaps the name leopard lily would more aptly apply to the decorative spots.

Spring thaw comes along to melt away deep winter snow in southeastern Washington's Klickitat Valley.

Daytime may come to an end but the old Pacific just keeps on churning and lashing at the foot of towering cliffs and mountains of the Na Pali Coastline on Kauai Island in Hawaii.